For: ~~Dennis Price~~

If your heart is wise, then my heart will be glad.

—Proverbs 23:15

From: Darren, Eric, Brent

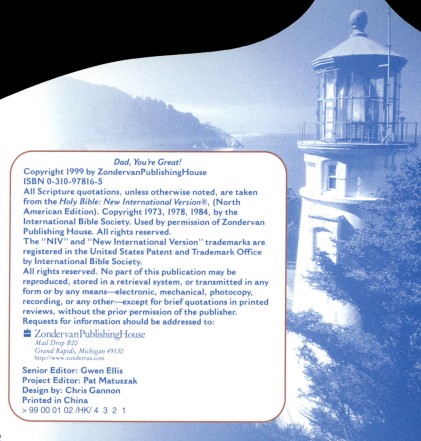

Dad, You're Great!
Copyright 1999 by ZondervanPublishingHouse
ISBN 0-310-97816-5
All Scripture quotations, unless otherwise noted, are taken from the *Holy Bible: New International Version®*, (North American Edition). Copyright 1973, 1978, 1984, by the International Bible Society. Used by permission of Zondervan Publishing House. All rights reserved.
The "NIV" and "New International Version" trademarks are registered in the United States Patent and Trademark Office by International Bible Society.
All rights reserved. No part of this publication may be reproduced, stored in a retrieval system, or transmitted in any form or by any means—electronic, mechanical, photocopy, recording, or any other—except for brief quotations in printed reviews, without the prior permission of the publisher.
Requests for information should be addressed to:

ZondervanPublishingHouse
Mail Drop B20
Grand Rapids, Michigan 49530
http://www.zondervan.com

Senior Editor: Gwen Ellis
Project Editor: Pat Matuszak
Design by: Chris Gannon
Printed in China
> 99 00 01 02 /HK/ 4 3 2 1

DAD
You're Great!

We have a gift for inspiration™

DAD
YOU'RE GREAT!

Surely I have a delightful inheritance.

—Psalm 16:6

DAD
You're Great!

By far the most valuable thing you can give your children is a loving relationship with you, their father.

—Paul Lewis

You're Great!

Be strong in the Lord and in his mighty power.

—Ephesians 6:10

DAD
You're Great!

It takes relational courage to build success in my marriage, with my kids or with my friends.

—Bill Hybels

DAD
You're Great!

God is love. Whoever lives in love lives in God, and God in him.

—1 John 4:16

You're Great!

When it comes to rearing children, there is a primary starting point: knowing your child.

—Charles R. Swindoll

DAD
YOU'RE GREAT!

Love one another
deeply, from the heart.

—1 PETER 1:22

YOU'RE GREAT!

The happiness of life is made up of minute fractions—
a kiss or smile, a kind look, a heartfelt compliment.

—William Scott

You're Great!

Jesus said, "But whoever drinks the water I give him will never thirst. Indeed, the water I give him will become in him a spring of water welling up to eternal life."

—John 4:14

DAD
You're Great!

The greatest and most productive purpose for living is to live to fulfill God's purpose for your life—to follow the manufacturer's recommendations for peak performance, to continue to press toward the mark of his high calling.

—Ken Davis

DAD
YOU'RE GREAT!

Trust in the LORD at all times . . . pour out your hearts to him, for God is our refuge.

—PSALM 62:8

You're Great!

The times demand big men. Not men who are big shots, but men who are big in heart and mind. Great men! Large-souled men!

—Richard Halverson

DAD
YOU'RE GREAT!

You have made known
to me the path of life.

—PSALM 16:11

DAD
You're Great!

A godly father is a man who understands what he means to his children, who is humbled by overwhelming joy over the impact he can make for God.

—Larry Crabb

Dad
You're Great!

I have set the LORD always
before me.
Because he is at my
right hand,
I will not be shaken.

—PSALM 16:8

DAD
You're Great!

I have examined America's breathless lifestyle and find it to be unacceptable. Why should we work ourselves into an early grave, missing those precious moments with loved ones who crave our affection and attention?

—James Dobson

DAD
YOU'RE GREAT!

I will praise the LORD, who counsels me;
even at night my heart instructs me.

—PSALM 16:7

You're Great!

Aristotle defined character as the decisions a person makes when the choice is not obvious. My father used to say, "Character is the way we act when nobody's looking."

—D. Bruce Lockerbie

DAD
YOU'RE GREAT!

He who has a wise
son delights in him.

—PROVERBS 23:24

You're Great!

The promises made, but not kept; the hopes dreamed, but not put into action—commitment matters. There is no success for a football player—or a Christian—without it.

—Reggie White

DAD
You're Great!

Lord, you establish peace for us; all that we have accomplished you have done for us.

—Isaiah 26:12

DAD
You're Great!

The work an unknown good man has done is like a vein of water flowing hidden underground, secretly making the ground green.

—Thomas Carlyle

DAD
YOU'RE GREAT!

I will give them singleness of heart and action . . . for their own good and the good of their children after them. I will make an everlasting covenant with them: I will never stop doing good to them, and I will inspire them.

—JEREMIAH 32:39–40

DAD
You're Great!

Even when we think we have lost that mustard seed of faith, we do well to remember that our Father is faithful, for he has loved us first.

—Philip W. Williams

DAD
You're Great!

The fruit of righteousness will be peace;
the effect of righteousness will be quietness and confidence forever.

—Isaiah 32:17

DAD
YOU'RE GREAT!

The believer's ministry is being Christ's person in the marketplace or the home, every moment of every day. This is the everyday business of holiness—the very nature of loving God.

—CHARLES COLSON

DAD
You're Great!

If any of you lacks wisdom, he should ask God, who gives generously to all without finding fault, and it will be given to him.

—James 1:5

You're Great!

Troubles are often the tools
by which God fashions
us for better things.

—Henry Ward Beecher

DAD
YOU'RE GREAT!

Look to the heavens:
 Who created all these?
He who brings out the starry host
 one by one,
 and calls them each by name.
Because of his great power and
 mighty strength,
 not one of them is missing.

—ISAIAH 40:26

You're Great!

Father! —To God himself we cannot give a holier name.

—William Wordsworth

You're Great!

So then, just as you received Christ Jesus as Lord, continue to live in him, rooted and built up in him, strengthened in the faith.

—Colossians 2:6–7

DAD
You're Great!

A Christian man is the most free lord of all, and subject to none; a Christian man is the most dutiful servant of all, and subject to everyone.

—Martin Luther

DAD
You're Great!

Those who hope in the LORD
 will renew their strength.
They will soar on wings like eagles;
 they will run and not grow
  weary,
 they will walk and not be faint.

—Isaiah 40:31

DAD
You're Great!

God gives to every man the virtue, temper, and understanding that lifts him into life and lets him fall just in the niche he was ordained to fall.

—WILLIAM COWPER

DAD
You're Great!

The man of integrity walks securely.

—Proverbs 10:9

You're Great!

The study of God's Word, for the purpose of discovering God's will, is the secret discipline which has formed the greatest characters.

—James W. Alexander

DAD
You're Great!

Whoever sows sparingly will also reap sparingly, and whoever sows generously will also reap generously.

—2 Corinthians 9:6

DAD
You're Great!

The soul cannot live without love. All depends on providing it with a worthy object. We can never love our neighbor too much.

—St. Francis de Sales

You're Great!

Imitate those who through faith and patience inherit what has been promised.

—Hebrews 6:12

DAD
You're Great!

A man who governs his passions is master of the world. We must either command them, or be enslaved by them. It is better to be a hammer than an anvil.

—St. Dominic

DAD
YOU'RE GREAT!

The word of God is
living and active.

—Hebrews 4:12

You're Great!

Jesus never asks anyone to do the impossible. With him all things are possible as we commit ourselves to his holy cause.

—Bob Briner

DAD
YOU'RE GREAT!

We are God's workmanship.

—Ephesians 2:10

DAD
You're Great!

It is a wise father that knows his own child.

—Shakespeare

DAD
You're Great!

"For I know the plans I have for you," declares the LORD, "plans to prosper you and not to harm you, plans to give you hope and a future."

—Jeremiah 29:11

DAD

You're Great!

This is true prayer: being all ears for God. The core of all prayer is indeed listening, obediently standing in the presence of God.

—Henri Nouwen

DAD
You're Great!

For God so loved the world that he gave his one and only Son, that whoever believes in him shall not perish but have eternal life.

—John 3:16

You're Great!

At the end of our life, we shall be judged by love.

—St. John of the Cross

DAD
You're Great!

For God did not send his Son into the world to condemn the world, but to save the world through him.

—John 3:17

DAD
You're Great!

God is not a deceiver, that he should offer to support us, and then, when we lean upon him, should slip away from us.

—St. Augustine

DAD
You're Great!

Where your treasure is,
there your heart will be also.

—Matthew 6:21

DAD
You're Great!

We have to be careful about what we want to improve in the world. Christ came to us to redirect our vision toward God in heaven and away from man-made gods.

—Christopher de Vinck

DAD
You're Great!

Clothe yourselves with compassion, kindness, humility, gentleness and patience. Bear with each other.

—Colossians 3:12–13

DAD
YOU'RE GREAT!

Only parents' love can last our lives.

—ROBERT BROWNING

DAD
You're Great!

There is a time for everything,
and a season for every activity under heaven.

—Ecclesiastes 3:1

DAD
You're Great!

It is not how much we have, but how much we enjoy, that makes happiness.

—Charles H. Spurgeon

DAD
You're Great!

The LORD has done great
things for us,
and we are filled with joy.

—Psalm 126:3

DAD
You're Great!

What do you do when you've painted yourself into a corner? Laugh! Laughter reduces tension and helps you regain control. Most of the problems you encounter in life aren't that serious.

—Robert Schuller

DAD
You're Great!

Forgetting what is behind and straining toward what is ahead, I press on toward the goal to win the prize for which God has called me heavenward in Christ Jesus.

—Philippians 3:13–14

You're Great!

Let us live, while
we are alive!

—Goethe

Dad

You're Great!

The fear of the LORD is the beginning of wisdom, and knowledge of the Holy One is understanding.

—Proverbs 9:10

DAD
You're Great!

People are generally called intelligent through a wrong use of this word. The intelligent are not those who have studied, but those whose soul is intelligent—who avoid what is evil and care for what is good.

—St. Anthony the Great

DAD
You're Great!

The crucible for silver and the furnace for gold, but man is tested by the praise he receives.

—Proverbs 27:21

DAD
You're Great!

The two hardest things to handle in life are failure and success.

—Unknown

Dad
You're Great!

Jesus said to them, "Watch out! Be on your guard against all kinds of greed; a man's life does not consist in the abundance of his possessions."

—Luke 12:15

DAD
You're Great!

The wealth of a man is the number of things which he loves and blesses, and which he is loved and blessed thereby.

—Thomas Carlyle

DAD
YOU'RE GREAT!

Let the word of Christ dwell in you richly as you teach and admonish one another with all wisdom, and as you sing . . . with gratitude in your hearts to God.

—COLOSSIANS 3:16

You're Great!

It is the heart that makes a man rich. He is rich according to what he is, not according to what he has.

—Henry Ward Beecher

DAD
You're Great!

God has said,
 "Never will I leave you;
  never will I forsake you."
So we say with confidence,
 "The Lord is my helper."

—Hebrews 13:5–6

You're Great!

Prayer does not change God,
but changes him who prays.

—Søren Kierkegaard

DAD
You're Great!

All Scripture is God-breathed . . . so that the man of God may be thoroughly equipped for every good work.

—2 Timothy 3:16–17

DAD
YOU'RE GREAT!

If I could have only one wish for God's people, it would be that all of us would return to the Word of God, that we would realize once and for all that His Book has the answers.

—CHARLES SWINDOLL

DAD
You're Great!

Jesus said, "I praise you, Father, Lord of heaven and earth, because you have hidden these things from the wise and learned, and revealed them to little children."

—Luke 10:21

DAD
You're Great!

Today take delight in the children. Share their enthusiasm for little things. Be like Christ and welcome the children.

—Christopher de Vinck

DAD
YOU'RE GREAT!

Let us not become weary in doing good, for at the proper time we will reap a harvest if we do not give up.

—GALATIANS 6:9

You're Great!

Firmness of purpose is one of the most necessary sinews of character and one of the best instruments of success.

—Lord Chesterfield

You're Great!

Be imitators of God, therefore, as dearly loved children and live a life of love, just as Christ loved us.

—Ephesians 5:1–2

DAD
You're Great!

Those who attain any excellence commonly spend life in one pursuit; for excellence is not often granted upon easier terms.

—Samuel Johnson

DAD
YOU'RE GREAT!

Enter his gates with thanksgiving
and his courts with praise;
give thanks to him and praise his
name.

—Psalm 100:4

You're Great!

Faith without thankfulness lacks strength and fortitude.

—John Henry Jowett

DAD
YOU'RE GREAT!

Small is the gate and narrow the road that leads to life, and only a few find it.

—Matthew 7:14

DAD

You're Great!

I have been driven many times to my knees by the overwhelming conviction that I had nowhere else to go.

—Abraham Lincoln

DAD
YOU'RE GREAT!

Who of you by worrying can add a single hour to his life?

—Matthew 6:27

You're Great!

We ought to act with God in the greatest simplicity, speaking to him frankly and plainly, and imploring his assistance in our affairs, just as they happen.

—Brother Lawrence

DAD
You're Great!

Many are the woes of the wicked, but the LORD's unfailing love surrounds the man who trusts in him.

—PSALM 32:10

You're Great!

The Lord takes note of our inner friction when hard times are oiled by tears.

—Charles R. Swindoll

DAD
You're Great!

O LORD, our Lord,
how majestic is your name in all
the earth!

—PSALM 8:1

You're Great!

Those who humbly admit their need for God's help and daily strength, will find that they have been granted the power of God.

JACK KUHATSCHEK

DAD
You're Great!

Many are the plans in a
man's heart,
but it is the LORD's purpose
that prevails.

—Proverbs 19:21

You're Great!

Dare to dream. Help our
children dream. Reach
out and take the dream
God has for you.

—Wintley Phipps

DAD
You're Great!

The LORD will be your confidence and will keep your foot from being snared.

—PROVERBS 3:26

You're Great!

Even when God leads you through difficult times, you won't find a more fulfilling life.

—Ken Davis

DAD
You're Great!

A man of knowledge uses words with restraint,
and a man of understanding is even-tempered.

—Proverbs 17:27

DAD
You're Great!

We must be more concerned with knowing Christ than with finding ourselves.

—Larry Crabb

You're Great!

And whatever you do, whether in word or deed, do it all in the name of the Lord Jesus.

—Colossians 3:17

You're Great!

It's not our skills or our know-how or our long experience that makes the biggest impact—we are the main message!

—Don Shula

DAD

You're Great!

Make it your ambition to lead a quiet life, to mind your own business and to work with your hands . . . so that your daily life may win the respect of outsiders.

—1 Thessalonians 4:11–12

You're Great!

Work as if everything depended upon work and pray as if everything depended on prayer.

—William Booth

DAD
YOU'RE GREAT!

Create in me a pure heart, O God,
and renew a steadfast spirit
within me. . . .
Restore to me the joy of your
salvation
and grant me a willing spirit, to
sustain me.

—PSALM 51:10,12

You're Great!

The things we do today—sowing seeds, or sharing simple truths of Christ—people will someday refer to as the first things that prompted them to think of Him.

—George Matheson

DAD
You're Great!

May the words of my mouth and
    the meditation of my heart
be pleasing in your sight,
O Lord, my Rock and my
    Redeemer.

—Psalm 19:14

You're Great!

He who labors as he prays lifts his heart to God with his hands.

—Bernard of Clairvaux

Dad
You're Great!

This is how we know what love is: Jesus Christ laid down his life for us. And we ought to lay down our lives for our brothers.

—1 John 3:16

DAD
YOU'RE GREAT!

Those who roll up their sleeves to advance God's kingdom give themselves away in love, so God and others might receive.

—BILL HYBELS

DAD
YOU'RE GREAT!

Jesus said, "Everyone who hears these words of mine and puts them into practice is like a wise man who built his house on the rock."

—MATTHEW 7:24

You're Great!

Measure your life—not by man's measurements but by God's measurements. Measure your life by your eternal investments.

—Wesley Duewel

DAD
You're Great!

We know that when Jesus appears, we shall be like him, for we shall see him as he is.

—1 John 3:2

DAD
You're Great!

Grant that love so pure
would change my life.

—Ken Gire

DAD
YOU'RE GREAT!

Find rest, O my soul, in God alone;
my hope comes from him.
He alone is my rock and my
salvation;
he is my fortress, I will not be
shaken.

—Psalm 62:5–6

You're Great!

Jesus declared war on the materialism of his day. And I would suggest he declares war on the materialism of our day as well.

—Richard J. Foster

You're Great!

Let us hold unswervingly to the hope we profess, for he who promised is faithful.

—HEBREWS 10:23

DAD
You're Great!

Be a beacon to those around you who are in the dark.

—Bob Briner

You're Great!

Let your conversation
be always full of grace.

—Colossians 4:6

YOU'RE GREAT!

The Spirit of God first imparts love; he next inspires hope, and then gives liberty.

—DWIGHT L. MOODY

DAD
You're Great!

Neither death nor life . . .
nor anything else in all creation,
will be able to separate us
from the love of God that is in
Christ Jesus our Lord.

—Romans 8:38–39

DAD
You're Great!

I challenge you each morning to get down on your knees and seek God's power to keep you a loving, humble, and effective leader or parent.

—Charles R. Swindoll

Dad
You're Great!

The Lord's servant must not quarrel; instead, he must be kind to everyone, able to teach, not resentful. Those who oppose him he must gently instruct.

—2 Timothy 2:24–25

You're Great!

Help me to realize that so much of true ministry is not what I schedule, but what comes as an intrusion to my schedule.

—Ken Gire

You're Great!

Keep on loving each other.

—Hebrews 13:1

DAD
You're Great!

"Practice senseless acts of beauty and random acts of kindness," is not quite a Christian ideal. Commit purposeful kindness in his name—actions of unstinting compassion and generosity that will reflect God's loving nature, vibrantly alive in us.

—Luci Shaw

DAD
You're Great!

Dear friends, since God so loved us, we also ought to love one another.

—1 John 4:11

You're Great!

Lord, you have made us for yourself, and our heart is restless until it rests in you.

—St. Augustine

DAD
You're Great!

Let the peace of Christ rule in your hearts. . . . And be thankful.

—Colossians 3:15

DAD

You're Great!

Have your heart right with Christ, and he will visit you often, and so turn weekdays into Sundays, meals into sacraments, homes into temples, and earth into heaven.

—Charles H. Spurgeon

DAD

YOU'RE GREAT!

SELECTIONS FROM

God's Words of Life from the Men's Devotional Bible, Grand Rapids, MI: Zondervan Publishing House, 1997.

God's Wisdom for Men Calendar, Grand Rapids, MI: Zondervan Publishing House, 1996.

Wisdom for Dads, Grand Rapids, MI: Zondervan Publishing House, 1996.